Photos from Liverpool, Manche and Carlisle

Chapter 1:Liverpool

Lusitania propeller, 1909

This propeller was one of four from passenger liner RMS *Lusitania* (1907). She sailed between Liverpool and New York until she was torpedoed by the German submarine U-20 on 7 May 1915 with the loss of 1,191 lives.

Lusitania and her sister ship *Mauretania* were owned by Liverpool's Cunard Line and carried passengers and mail on regular services to the USA. *Lusitania* held the Blue Riband for the fastest crossing of the Atlantic by a passenger vessel, making the journey in under 4.5 days. This propeller was fitted in 1909 to improve her speed.

Lusitania continue[...]
outbreak of the Fi[...]
under twenty min[...]
Ireland. People we[...]
targeting of a pas[...]
still causes contro[...]

The *Lusitania: [...]*
Merseyside Mar[...]
of the ship and h[...]
marks the anniv[...]
commemorativ[...]

Well, from Liverpool museums window...

Chapter 2: Manchester

Statues,outside Piccadilly station

Manchester Cathedral and pigeon

Manchester Cathedral

Manchester Cathedral and a piece of the Ghandi statue

Chester, a few photos.

Chester Cathedral

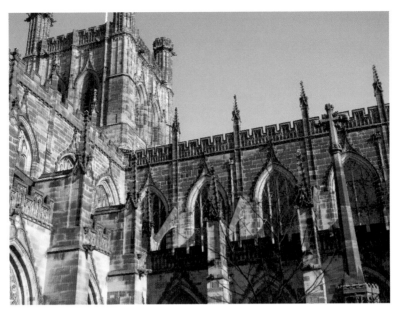

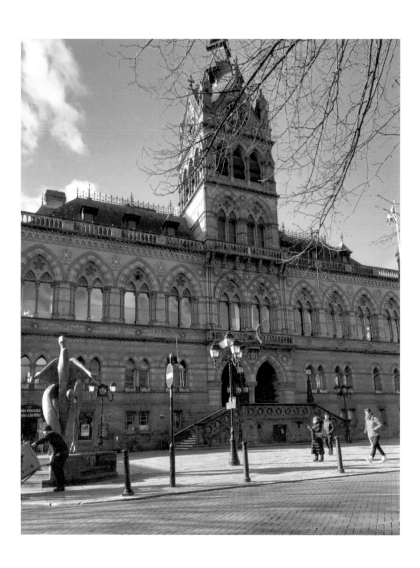

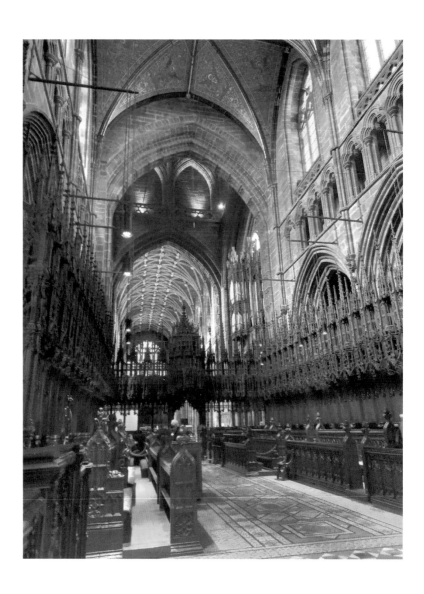

Carlisle, a few photos

Carlisle castle, which is mostly closed as it is
in use..

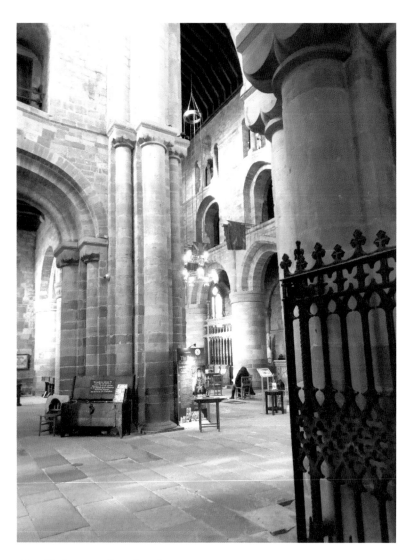

Carlisle cathedral

Carlisle Cathedral

Carlisle cathedral, so beautiful

This is tourist information, I think

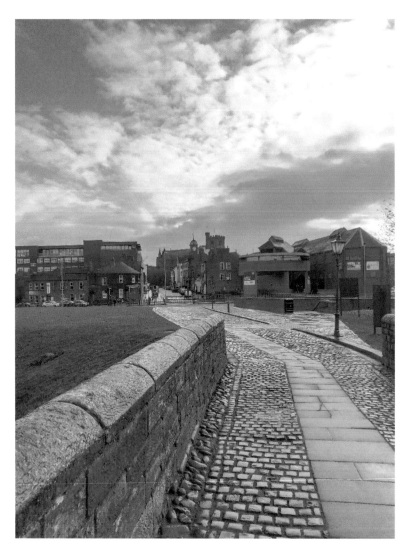

This is just a few photos from different cities/towns. And during autumn and late winter.

Will visit again spring or summer.

I also have photos on picfair.com

Printed in Great Britain
by Amazon

79741862R00038